THE FACTS ABOUT

DRUG
TESTING

BY
Judy Monroe

EDITED BY
Laurie Beckelman

CONSULTANT
Elaine Wynne, M.A., Licensed Psychologist

CRESTWOOD HOUSE

New York

LIBRARY OF CONGRESS CATALOGING IN PUBLICATION DATA

Monroe, Judy.
  The facts about drug testing

  p.   cm. — (The Facts about)
  SUMMARY: Discusses all aspects of testing for drugs in a person's body, including types of
tests and their results.
  1. Drug testing — United States — Juvenile literature. [1. Drug testing.] I. Title. II. Series.
HV5823.5.U5M66   1990   362.29'164—dc20   89-25425   CIP
ISBN 0-89686-492-8   AC

PHOTO CREDITS

Cover: The Image Works: John Griffin
AP – Wide World: 4, 10, 13, 23, 37, 39
Photo Researchers: (Richard Hutchings) 7, 42; (Borrfdon/Explorer) 16
Devaney Stock Photos: (Ken Cole) 8; 26
DRK Photo: (Randy Trine) 15; (N.H. Cheatham) 28-29; (Allan Kaye) 30; (Don & Pat
Valenti) 32
The Image Works: (John Griffin) 19, 21; (Bob Daemmrich) 35

Macmillan Publishing Company
866 Third Avenue
New York, NY 10022
Collier Macmillan Canada, Inc.

CRESTWOOD HOUSE

Printed in the United States of America
First Edition
10 9 8 7 6 5 4 3 2 1

TABLE OF CONTENTS

LOST GOLD

Remember Ben Johnson, the Canadian sprinter in the 1988 Olympics? On September 25, he set a new world record in the 100-meter race in Seoul, South Korea. But two days later, he was disqualified from the Olympics.

Ben Johnson was the first track and field winner stripped of his gold medal. He had used an *anabolic steroid,* a drug some people think builds muscles and strength. But anabolic steroids also damage the heart and liver and cause other health problems. And taking them before an athletic competition is *illegal.* They are against the law.

Drug testing showed that there were anabolic steroids in Ben Johnson's urine. A drug test analyzes what is in urine or blood. The urine or blood is treated with chemicals. Changes in color or other reactions occur if drugs are there. From these changes, laboratory workers can tell what drugs are present.

Drug testing is used in schools, homes, and work places, as well as in sports. In fact, drug testing is a big business. In 1988, drug tests cost American companies $200 million!

But drug testing raises many questions. Does it work? Which tests work the best? Why did drug testing start? And most important of all: Should drug testing be used?

Ben Johnson raises his arm in victory as he crosses the finish line at the Seoul Olympics. Two days later, when tests showed drugs in his system, the gold medal was taken away from him.

5

BEGINNINGS

Drug testing started in drug treatment centers as a way to test addicts. In 1970, the Department of Defense began a drug testing program to find and treat *heroin* users. At this time, some soldiers returning from Vietnam were heroin addicts.

Then government interest in drug testing dropped. But people were still concerned, so studies were done. A 1976 study of sailors found that one out of five used illegal drugs. Another found that a third of all seamen used *marijuana*. At the same time, the number of deaths from heroin overdoses had started to grow among U.S. soldiers in Europe.

This was scary news. Congress debated whether or not drug testing was a good way to fight drug abuse. But nothing happened until 1981.

Then, the Armed Forces Institute of Pathology began testing employees' urine for marijuana. The program identified drug users and helped them get free of drugs. The idea caught on outside the military. Airline, railroad, and aerospace companies set up drug testing programs. Big businesses and sports organizations like the Olympics soon followed.

Some people think that drug testing programs are the answer to getting help for drug users. Others fear that such programs will invade privacy and result in punishment, not help, for those found to use drugs. Some people feel so strongly that they have filed suits that test the legality of drug testing programs.

ILLEGAL DRUG USE

"Some of the guys want me to use *cocaine* before games or at parties," said Chris, age 12. "I won't. But I wonder how many people use it or other drugs."

The use of illegal drugs is at an all-time high. The American Council for Drug Education estimates that 23 million Americans aged 12 and over use them. Sales of

One out of four Americans has smoked marijuana, even though it is an illegal drug.

illegal drugs top $100 billion a year. That's more than the annual income of all American farmers combined.

Three widely used illegal drugs are heroin, marijuana, and cocaine. About 500,000 Americans use heroin. About 25 percent, or one out of four, have tried marijuana. Today, more than 25 million people use it.

But cocaine use is catching up with marijuana use. More than 21 million Americans have tried cocaine. Between 5 and 6 million use it often. Americans use over 150 tons of cocaine each year!

All drugs cause mental and physical changes in people. Most illegal drugs are too powerful for medical use and often change a person's moods or feelings. Illegal drugs are used without a doctor's permission.

DRUG ABUSE, HEALTH, AND CRIME

Drug abuse is a big health problem in the United States. *Addiction* to most illegal drugs is easy to acquire. Addiction is a physical and emotional need for something. Someone who is addicted to cocaine feels a need for cocaine, for example.

Besides addiction, drug abuse results in diseases, disabilities, and even death. A recent report from the U.S. Department of Justice found these three alarming facts: One

A dramatic display of cocaine and a death's head. A razor for cutting coke and a straw for sniffing it into the nose are also shown.

out of four hospital admissions is from drug abuse. Forty percent, or two out of five, of all accidents that result in hospitalization are because of drugs. And the national cost of all accidents from drug abuse is $41 billion per year.

Crime and violence also result from drug abuse. Addicts often steal to get money for more drugs. A government report found that heroin addicts commit at least 100,000 burglaries, robberies, and auto thefts each day. Joseph Califano, Jr., former secretary of the federal Department of Health, Education, and Welfare (now Health and Human Services), estimated that 200,000 burglaries, robberies, and auto thefts are committed each day by addicts alone!

Federal and city drug enforcers try to stop illegal drug sales in cities and towns. Government officers try to stop the smuggling of illegal drugs into the United States. But their efforts have not worked very well.

America's largest city, New York City, is an example of a city waging war on drugs. The cost is high. In 1989, Mayor Edward Koch said the "$250 million spent annually by the city to combat drug dealers does not buy enough police, courts, and drug-education workers to dent the problem."

So people look for other solutions. Many think drug testing is one answer and that it can help prevent drug abuse.

Police arresting suspected drug dealers

JAR WARS

Speaking of drug testing, 12-year-old Linda said: "If it's used all over—in sports, schools, and workplaces—I think it will help stop drug abuse. "My brother Joe just tested positive for cocaine while on his job. He's in a treatment program now and is glad to get help."

Some people agree with Linda that drug testing is all right. But others disagree. This clash of views over drug testing is called Jar Wars. This phrase came from the practice of collecting urine in bottles for testing.

Many employers say drug testing has helped them get drugs out of their workplaces. Drug-free workers miss fewer workdays and have fewer accidents. If workers like Joe test positive, they can get treatment.

Others say that drug testing is a form of prevention. It helps combat peer pressure. If you know you will be tested for drugs, it is easier to say no to taking drugs in the first place.

But others think that even if drug testing prevents drug abuse, its costs outweigh its benefits. The Fourth Amendment of the Constitution says, "The right of the people to be secure in their persons, houses, papers, and effects, against unreasonable searches and seizures, shall not be violated…." The people against drug testing believe this means that general searches of people are unfair and unreasonable. So drug testing is a violation of privacy.

Some think drug testing is unfair. Drug tests are not

Drug testing and drug abuse arouse strong feelings. Here people rally in support of a successful drug treatment center – Daytop Village.

always accurate. This means that someone who is drug free can be accused of taking drugs. Also, drug tests require people to prove that they do not use drugs. Some consider this unfair – that it goes against American law, which says that you should be considered innocent until proven guilty.

Drug tests do not measure job performance. They cannot show if someone was high at the time of the sample.

Urine may test positive for drugs that were taken long before the sample was given. So some people feel that what they do on their own time is no one else's business.

To some people, drug testing says your bosses, your parents, or your schools do not trust you.

Jar Wars clashes often result in legal battles. Some courts have found in favor of drug testing. Those courts that strike down drug-testing programs usually think such testing violates the Fourth Amendment.

TODAY'S ILLEGAL DRUGS

Many drug tests analyze for the four groups of illegal drugs used in the United States today. They are *stimulants, opiates, sedatives,* and *hallucinogens.*

The best-known group is the stimulants. These drugs excite the body. They speed up the nervous system and increase the activity of the mind and body. They make people feel peppy.

Cocaine, *crack,* and *amphetamines* are stimulants. Users like the fast and intense "high" they get from these drugs. When Tom sniffed cocaine at a friend's party, it reached his brain within three minutes. He felt excited and happy. But an hour later, the cocaine wore off and he felt tired, dull, tense, and edgy.

Crack is a powerful form of cocaine. It is often smoked and gives the most dramatic cocaine high. When Janet

14   *A model demonstrates how cocaine is snorted. His straw is a $20 bill.*

smokes crack, she feels happy in seconds. But 15 to 20 minutes later, she feels down or depressed.

Sue uses amphetamines to stay alert when she studies for tests. Amphetamine highs often are not as intense as cocaine or crack highs. But all three drugs do harmful things to your body.

They speed up normal body functions. Blood vessels narrow, so the heart works faster. The heart rate and breathing quicken, and blood pressure rises. Weak blood vessels can burst and a weak heart can begin skipping heartbeats. This may lead to a heart attack or death.

Opiates and sedatives, or downers, cause the opposite to happen to the body. They tend to relax people. Users may have a fast "rush" of good feelings. But bad feelings soon follow, along with nausea, vomiting, and restlessness. Sometimes, people feel sleepy. Large doses or longtime use can cause death.

Heroin is the best-known opiate. It can be smoked, but more often is injected with needles into people's blood vessels. If needles are dirty, there may be other dangers – disease, such as *AIDS*, for instance.

Some people use hallucinogens like marijuana, *LSD*, and *PCP.* Hallucinogens cause vivid feelings and thoughts. They change people's moods. No one can predict whether he or she will feel happy or sad on them.

Hallucinogens can make people feel calm and relaxed. Time seems to move slowly. At other times, they may feel tense, anxious, and even afraid. Their feelings and thoughts are often distorted while taking hallucinogens, so they may do harmful things to themselves or others.

17

Some students use amphetamines so they can cram for exams without sleeping. The drug speeds up the heart rate and breathing and can cause heart attacks.

TYPES OF DRUG TESTS

"Drug tests don't hurt," laughed Karen, age 13. She is on the swimming team. "I went to the bathroom and urinated into a little bottle. That's it. But I felt a little funny walking through the locker room with my urine!"

More and more drug tests are done each year. In 1985, about 5 million drug tests were done. By 1988, American laboratories had run 15 to 20 million drug tests. About half were for businesses. The rest were for prisons, the police, and public treatment programs.

Drug tests work because most drugs stay in a person's urine for two to five days or more. The amount of time varies. Cocaine lasts three days, and heroin and PCP stay for four days. Marijuana can stay for up to two weeks, but usually disappears after five days.

Traces, or small amounts, of these and other drugs can be found in both your blood and urine. Urine works best for drug testing. Drugs are ten times more concentrated in urine than in blood. And drug traces remain in urine much longer.

Each drug test starts the same way, like Karen's. First, a small amount of urine is put into a glass or plastic bottle. This is a sample. The bottle is sealed and labeled. The sample is closely watched so that the person being tested cannot tamper with it. Some companies sell sealed plastic bottles of drug-free urine!

Laboratory scientists test urine samples with one of four methods. The *enzyme immunoassay* is the most common drug-testing method. The Syva Company is the leader in this, with its EMIT test. EMIT can test for more than ten drugs, including marijuana, cocaine, and amphetamines. The tests don't cost much—less than ten dollars each—and are fast.

For an EMIT test, a urine sample is broken into ten

One of the machines that detects drugs in urine

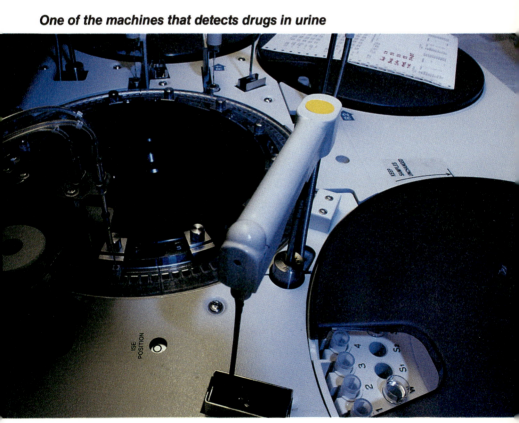

smaller samples, one for each drug. Then each is mixed with different *antibodies*. Antibodies are substances made by the blood that fight off foreign organisms. If drugs attach to the antibodies, the urine changes a different color for different drugs. The color changes tell laboratory people which drugs are in the urine.

Radioimmunoassay (RIA) drug tests are like EMIT. The urine sample is also mixed with antibodies that attach to illegal drugs. But in RIA, antibodies have *radioactive* chemicals attached. Radioactive chemicals give off radiation that is seen by a machine. If no drugs are in the sample, no radiation is given off.

The most popular RIA test is Abuscreen, the military's preferred drug test. RIA requires more complex machines and more training for laboratory people than does EMIT. But the military likes RIA because it is faster than EMIT.

Thin layer chromatography (TLC) costs less than either EMIT or RIA. A single test can find up to 40 drugs in one urine sample. But the results are not measured by a machine. Instead, trained lab people decide what the TLC results mean. So results from a urine sample may vary from lab to lab.

In TLC, a glass plate is covered with a thin layer of gel, a jellylike substance. A small dot of urine is placed near one edge of the gel. The glass plate is then placed upright in a container. After a period of time, the original spot is gone and a series of spots appear all over the gel. Each spot is a different drug that separated from the urine.

The best and most accurate way to test for drugs today is

Test tubes of urine lined up to be checked for opiates

with *gas chromatography/mass spectrometry* (GC/MS), which uses $100,000 machines. GC/MS results are very accurate—99.9 percent! Most courts of law accept these drug tests.

GC/MS uses a gas, special chemicals, and electric charges to separate the different chemicals in a urine sample. Drugs, which are chemicals, separate from other parts of the urine. The test is complex and costs a lot—$40 to $70 each. Highly trained lab people must run the machines and analyze the results.

Because GC/MS machines cost so much, most places don't have them. The machines are also big and hard to move around from labs to factories. Many places use the EMIT or RIA tests instead because they are fast and don't cost a lot.

DO DRUG TESTS WORK?

In 1988, the Olympic Committee in Seoul, South Korea, said that British runner Linford Christie failed a drug test. He would have to give up his silver medal. But the committee soon changed its decision, and Christie kept his award. What happened?

After winning the running event, Christie was tested for illegal drugs. One was found. Christie protested and other tests were run. The new tests showed that the drug in his urine was not illegal. It had come from ginseng tea, a type of herb tea.

Linford Christie's case is not unusual. Up to 10 percent of drug tests, or one out of ten, are not correct. They come out positive for illegal drugs even though the person has taken none. This means that out of 100 people who are drug-free, ten will be positive in drug tests. At other times, drug tests don't identify people who are taking illegal drugs.

The RIA and EMIT tests are not as accurate as the GC/MS test. They have more errors. Researchers agree that positive urine tests should be retested with GC/MS. But that costs more money, takes extra time, and not all places have access to GC/MS machines or labs. So retests may not be done.

Human mistakes are another reason drug tests sometimes don't work correctly. Suppose your urine sample gets mixed up with another person's. Or maybe the bottles

22 *Linford Christie, in blue, strides into his victory at the Olympics. Like Ben Johnson, Christie was later accused of using drugs until it was discovered that the "drug" was really tea.*

weren't cleaned well, and a small bit from someone else's urine got into yours. Sometimes laboratory people are not well trained and make mistakes.

Tim Witherspoon knows about human mistakes in drug testing. A few years ago, James "Bonecrusher" Smith won a heavyweight fight against Tim Witherspoon. After the fight, Witherspoon's urine was tested. It showed he had

used marijuana. Witherspoon protested, so a check was made. His test actually showed he had not taken illegal drugs before the fight. His results had been reported as positive because someone had misread his numbers.

Some foods, such as poppy seeds, can result in a positive drug test. These small, round, black seeds are sprinkled on rolls and bagels. They contain tiny amounts of morphine. Eating three poppy-seed bagels may give you a positive result on the RIA and EMIT tests.

Some legal drugs are chemically like illegal drugs, which means that drug tests can't tell them apart. This means some legal drugs show positive on drug tests. A few years ago, 100 members of a football team had EMIT tests. Thirty-five tested positive for marijuana. But retests found that all had taken ibuprofen, a legal painkiller similar to aspirin. The problem? Ibuprofen's chemistry is like that of marijuana. EMIT tests were corrected for this problem.

A few prescription drugs (drugs given by doctors) and diet aids give positive EMIT and RIA test results, too. For example, EMIT and RIA tests can't tell heroin and codeine apart. Codeine is in many cough syrups. Some herbal teas, such as Linford Christie's ginseng tea, give positive cocaine results.

Drug tests pose another problem. People whose urine has traces of an illegal drug may not have used the drug for a while. Marijuana can stay in the body for several weeks. A positive test may not mean a person used marijuana recently.

The best drug tests can tell only that someone has used an illegal drug. They can't tell how much of the drug was taken or when. They can't test for drug addiction. "Testing," said Dr. Ronald Seigel of the UCLA School of Medicine, "does only one thing. It detects what is being tested."

MYTHS AND TRUTHS

Tim, age 12, tried cocaine with his friends for the first time on Saturday. "And this is my only time," he told them. "I don't like this stuff."

But he worried on Monday. He'd forgotten about the drug test after school. Could he get the cocaine out of his body? Friends told him:

"Drink lots of water. It washes out drugs."

"Drink lemon juice or vinegar. They hide drugs."

"Add salt or Drano to your urine sample."

Fearful test-takers, like Tim, try many things to get a clean drug test. None work. Drug tests are becoming more and more accurate and can detect very small amounts of drugs. Home "cures" don't hide, wash out, or dilute illegal drugs.

Some people take other drugs to hide an illegal drug. At the 1985 Pan American Games in Indianapolis, six athletes were thrown out for using an illegal drug. They had used *probenecid,* which hides traces of anabolic steroids in urine.

Chrissy, age 14, wondered, "The room was thick with marijuana smoke at last night's party. I didn't smoke any. But will I test positive for marijuana because I breathed it?" Researchers find that people like Chrissy, who inhale marijuana but do not smoke it, do not test positive.

ATHLETES AND ILLEGAL DRUGS

Some athletes, like Ben Johnson in the 1988 Olympics, look for ways to gain advantages. They think more and better training is not enough. Sometimes they try to gain that edge by using illegal drugs.

Athletes use illegal drugs for other reasons. Remember Len Bias, the Maryland basketball star drafted in the first round by a pro team? He threw a big party to celebrate. A friend brought cocaine, and Bias took some. But the cocaine sped up his heart too fast and Bias died from a heart attack.

Many owners and managers of professional teams and coaches of college teams think drugs are their number one problem. They hope testing will stop drug abuse. Some players, unions, and associations are against drug testing. They think it violates their human rights because it invades their privacy. Other players think drug testing is all right—as long as drug treatment and education are given to those with positive tests.

A lot of athletes think they can build up their bodies with anabolic steroids. Doctors say steroids actually tear the body down.

COLLEGE SPORTS

Ron's dream had come true. He had won a football scholarship to his first-choice college. While warming up on the field, he was called into the coach's office.

These college football players can be tested for drugs anytime without warning.

"Ron, you have to take two drug tests," said the coach. "One's for the school, and you won't be able to compete without taking it. The other is for the National Collegiate Athletic Association. You'll have to take them before you take part in the national championships."

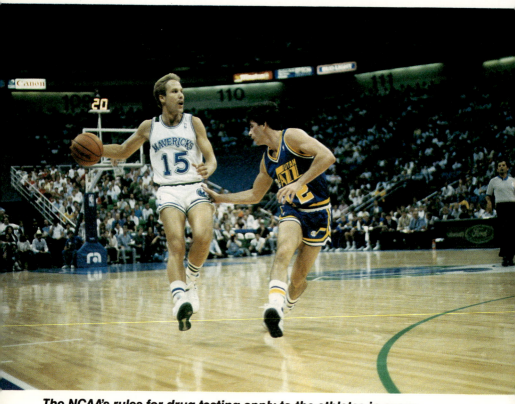

The NCAA's rules for drug testing apply to the athletes in every college sport.

"I don't use drugs," responded Ron.

"Good," replied the coach. "But all college athletes must take them."

In January 1986, the National Collegiate Athletic Association (NCAA) began a drug-testing program for college athletes. The program is for athletes who play in NCAA championship events and in post-season games. The drug tests are random. This means athletes can be tested at any time and without warning. They can be tested before, during, or after an NCAA game.

The 86 banned drugs on the NCAA list include illegal drugs and others, such as anabolic steroids. Under NCAA rules, if you test positive for anabolic steroids, for example, you are suspended for at least 90 days and can't compete. All college athletes sign a consent form for the NCAA program. If they don't, they can't compete in college games.

The program was begun to ensure that no student has an unfair edge over others because of drugs. Also, the NCAA thinks this program helps student athletes avoid drug abuse.

PRO SPORTS

Some professional sports leagues have drug-testing programs, too. Baseball began *random drug testing* in July 1985 in the minor leagues and among major league field managers and umpires. Since 1986, the program has included all baseball players except those in unions.

Said baseball commissioner Peter Ueberroth, "Drug testing is a proven deterrent to use and an effective tool. It is definitely not a sole solution." Commissioner Ueberroth knows that testing alone would not help drug abusers stop. So, the baseball program counsels and treats players who test positive.

Football commissioner Pete Rozelle long wanted to take action against drugs in sports. In some circles, he said, cocaine "had replaced candy and flowers in the dating process."

So in July 1986, Pete Rozelle began a random drug testing program of all National Football League (NFL) players. In this program, there are two random urine tests per player in the regular football season. A first-time positive result brings a 30-day counseling and testing period. A second positive test means a 30-day suspension at half pay. If athletes get a third positive test, they can't play pro football.

"More than 2,500 players were tested during 1988 training camp," said a spokesperson for the NFL. They were tested for five groups of illegal drugs and for alcohol. The NFL also began testing for anabolic steroids in 1987. Players with positive drug tests get treatment and counseling.

In July 1989, The Athletics Congress, the national group for track and field, started year-round drug testing. The top 25 athletes in each event can be randomly tested during the year.

The National Hockey League and the National Basketball Association (NBA) don't have drug-testing programs. But, since 1983, under an agreement with the players, the NBA can test when there is "reasonable cause."

Professional football players can be tested twice a season for drugs. Players with three positive tests can be banned from professional sports forever.

OLYMPICS

The Olympics' first brush with drug use came in the 1960 summer games in Rome. Danish cyclist Knud Jensen fainted in a race and died. He had taken an illegal stimulant before the race. A concerned Olympics Committee studied how to control drug abuse and began drug testing in 1968.

In the 1983 Pan American Games, 19 athletes were thrown out for taking illegal drugs. The next year, in the Los Angeles Olympics, 11 tested positive for anabolic steroids and could not compete. Since then, other athletes who have taken illegal drugs have not been allowed to compete in the Olympics. Or, like Ben Johnson, they haven't been allowed to keep their medals.

By drug testing, the Olympic Committee gives a clear message that "to win at any price" is not all right. Also, the Committee said, "using drugs to increase performance is unethical." It's the same as cheating.

AT SCHOOL

A school district in Wisconsin has a drug testing program for students suspected of drug use. If you refuse to take the test, you're suspended for three days. If you test positive, you can get treatment.

At Edison High School, in Huntington Beach, California, students can join a drug-testing program. It's their choice. The program runs year-round. If results are positive, students can decide if they want to get treatment.

In Bellaire, Ohio, all high school athletes and cheerleaders get tested for drugs. All students get drug testing if they go to Hamilton County High School in Jasper, Florida.

Even though many U.S. schools have drug-testing programs, some students, school officials, and parents don't like them. These people think that parents are responsible for their children, not the schools. They are also concerned about possible misuse of testing. For example, schools might use positive tests against troublemakers. Or a teacher could unfairly grade students who showed positive.

In some schools, students who refuse to take drug tests are suspended. At this junior high in Texas, that means sitting at a desk in a cinder block cubicle all day.

The National Federation of State High School Associations "does not promote drug testing in the nation's schools." If schools want drug testing, that's their choice, says the National Federation. This organization represents 20,000 high schools across America.

Some schools have *mandatory drug-testing* programs. But the courts usually find these programs illegal, and the schools are told they cannot have them. The main argument against drug testing in schools is that it violates the Fourth Amendment to the Constitution. This law says that general searches of people are unfair and unreasonable. So the courts have often ruled that mandatory drug testing in schools is unfair because all students must undergo drug testing.

What is the best choice for schools? Some say mandatory drug testing. Some say no drug testing. Still others believe that a voluntary drug testing program, like the one at Edison High School, is best.

IN THE MILITARY

"Listen up, soldiers. When your life depends on the catlike reflexes and bullmoose strength of your buddies, you don't want them strung out on drugs. If they're thinking they can get around the army's drug-testing program, they're wrong," said an article in *Soldier,* an army magazine.

Drug-free military people are vital to America's security, says the military. So, the armed forces give over 3 million drug tests each year to soldiers, sailors, and marines. The navy gives more drug tests than any other organization in the United States. The military tests find six types of illegal drugs – cocaine, marijuana, amphetamines, sedatives, opiates, and PCP. The program costs over $47 million a year.

Urine testing of all military people began in 1981. Since then, drug taking in the military appears to have decreased. A survey showed that between 1980 and 1985, drug abuse in the military dropped from 27 percent to 9 percent. Random drug testing has been upheld in military courts, too.

The U.S. military began testing for drugs in 1981. The combination of soldiers using drugs and weapons could be deadly.

Before entering the military, recruits must sign a contract. It says they will not use drugs and that they will be tested for drugs while in the service. Each branch of the military sets its own policy for deciding who is tested.

Each commander chooses how to test troops—as a group or one by one. The commander also decides what to do with those who test positive. Commanders often refer these people to local treatment centers.

IN THE GOVERNMENT

It was a cold Sunday afternoon, January 4, 1987. At 1:30 P.M., near Baltimore, Maryland, two trainmen did not stop at warning signals. They drove a string of three 130-ton Conrail freight trains into the path of a crowded Amtrak passenger train from Washington. Sixteen people died, and 176 were injured.

The engineer of the Conrail trains said he had been smoking marijuana while running the train. His urine test was positive. The brakeman also had smoked marijuana just before the accident.

Angry people wanted to know why this happened. Congress had passed an antidrug bill in 1986. Why wasn't it working? This bill allowed tougher penalties for drug crimes and tighter enforcement of drug laws. It also allowed the government to begin testing workers in sensitive jobs for drugs. But many federal agencies did not yet have drug testing programs.

Finally, in November 1988, the Department of Transportation (DOT) began random drug testing. The DOT program covers 4 million transportation workers in *sensitive jobs*—jobs that involve the safety and security of others. These are people who operate railroads, buses, trucks, and airplanes.

So far, the U.S. Supreme Court has upheld these drug-testing laws. The Court believes that the public's right to safety outweighs the workers' rights to privacy under the Fourth Amendment. For example, in March 1989, the Supreme Court said railroads can give drug tests after an accident or after a safety violation. It also said the U.S. Customs Service can test workers in sensitive and

A drug test revealed that the engineer of this train had been smoking marijuana just before it crashed.

weapon-carrying jobs. The Federal Aviation Administration has had drug testing for air traffic controllers since 1987.

Court cases have upheld testing of police and correction officers, too. In 1986, the New York State Supreme Court said officers who drive prison vans and buses for the city could be tested. Workers who move prisoners must provide security and safety, said the Court.

A recent survey by the National Institute of Justice found that about 75 percent of police departments required drug tests for job applicants. Almost all departments approved drug testing of police officers suspected of illegal drug use.

IN BUSINESS

"I applied for a job at DuPont, the giant chemical company," said Jenny, age 22. She's a chemist. "I got it. The other two lost out because they tested positive for marijuana."

By 1989, almost half of all major U.S. companies had some or all job applicants, like Jenny, tested for drugs. Besides DuPont, others are IBM, Kodak, 3M, AT&T, Lockheed, Westinghouse, Federal Express, Exxon, the *New York Times,* General Motors, Union Carbide, Toyota Motor Sales USA, TWA, and Greyhound. Most companies won't hire you if you test positive.

A drug-free company provides a safe, healthy, and productive place for workers. Drug testing, say businesses, screens out potential problems. But drug testing costs a lot. Experts estimate that by 1991, businesses will spend $500 million.

But drug abuse costs businesses a lot, too. A Department of Labor report said, "People don't check their *substance abuse* problems at the door when they enter the workplace." Drug abusers are absent from the job up to 16 times as often as drug-free workers. They also take three times as many sick days and have nearly four times the number of accidents. Lost work time means that employees aren't producing for the company.

The National Institute on Drug Abuse said one in five workers aged 18 to 25 uses drugs on the job. The Institute also found that one in eight workers aged 26 to 34 uses drugs on the job.

Which employees should be tested for drugs? There is no clear answer. Some public safety workers undergo random testing. The Nuclear Regulatory Commission is drawing up rules for random testing of power plant operators. Other businesses test when they have reasonable cause to believe a worker abuses drugs. The courts have not yet ruled on whether business employees can be required to be in drug-testing programs.

Some people already used drugs before starting a new job. But that's not always true. Sometimes people start using drugs after they get their jobs. Perhaps they are bored with their jobs and turn to drugs. Thomas E. Backer, president

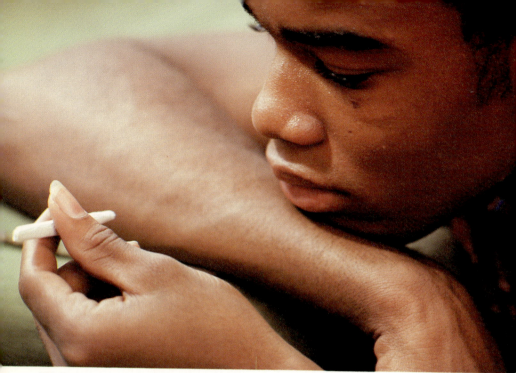

While this teen thinks about smoking marijuana, his parents may be thinking about a home testing kit.

of the Human Interaction Research Institute in Los Angeles, said on-the-job stress leads to many drug abuse problems. "Self-medication for stress is the single most common reason for abuse of drugs in the workplace," he said.

Some cities and states have drug-testing programs for their employees. San Francisco was the first city to have drug testing, back in 1985. Other cities now have similar programs that test only if there is reasonable belief that a worker uses drugs on the job. If a job applicant's drug test is positive, states such as Minnesota, Connecticut, and Vermont require that the results be sent directly to the applicant. This is because most employers don't explain why you didn't get a job.

Many companies have *Employee Assistance Programs* (EAP) to prevent and help with drug abuse in the workplace. The larger the company, the more likely it is to have a drug-testing program or an EAP. To help businesses, the National Institute on Drug Abuse set up a Workplace Helpline and a toll-free number. It is listed below in "For More Information."

HOME TESTING

The story was going around Jefferson Elementary. "Did you hear about Owen? His parents think he takes drugs, so they tested him at home!"

In July 1986, a home testing kit called Aware, made by American Drug Screens, came out. For under $25, a parent gets a urine sample bottle, a mailing tube, and a lab test. After the child urinates into the bottle, the parent caps it and mails it to American Drug Screens. Two weeks later, the results arrive in the mail.

Peter True thinks home drug testing is useful. He is the president of Kids Saving Kids. This is a Lancaster, Pennsylvania, group of teenagers who teach schoolchildren the dangers of drugs. Such a kit, he said, helps parents face the facts of drug abuse.

The people of Cobb County, Georgia, also agree. In June 1985, many hospitals and institutes there began a low-cost drug-testing program open to all people in Cobb County. It gives drug abuse results to parents privately.

Under this program, parents bring a sample of their child's urine to a Cobb County hospital. About a week later, parents call the office to get the results. The parent's only cost is the lab test, which is about $35.

But others disagree with the value of home testing. Dr. Joe Sanders, a pediatrician, thinks that guilty children might add things to the sample to try to hide illegal drugs. Also, some drugs don't show up in the test because the child took them weeks before.

Some people think drug testing by parents hurts the relationship between parent and child. Children may think their parents do not trust them. Other people believe that parents who use drug tests on their children won't talk to them about the dangers of drug use. They think it is not enough to give children drug tests, then put them into treatment if the tests are positive. Prevention is the key, they say, and parents should communicate this to their children.

Lloyd Johnston, a University of Michigan researcher, disagrees. The threat of a home test gives kids a good reason to refuse drugs, he said.

You'll have to make up your own mind about drug testing. Who gains from testing? Should it be used by businesses or the government? What about in schools or at home?

FOR MORE INFORMATION

For more information about drug testing, contact:

National Federation of State High School Associations
800-366-6667

Workplace Helpline
800-843-4971

U.S. Olympic Committee
800-233-0393

American Council on Drug Education
5820 Hubbard Drive
Rockville, MD 20852

National Collegiate Athletic Association
Nall Avenue at 63rd Street
P.O. Box 6620
Mission, KS 66201

National Institute on Drug Abuse
5600 Fishers Lane
Rockville, MD 20857

GLOSSARY/INDEX

ADDICTION—*Drug dependence; a physical and emotional need for a substance.* 9, 24

AIDS—*Acquired Immune Deficiency Syndrome; a disease that destroys the ability of the body's immune system to protect itself.* 17

AMPHETAMINES—*Drugs that excite the body and give people pep.* 14, 17, 19, 37

ANABOLIC STEROIDS—*Drugs that are thought to build and strengthen muscles. They also damage the heart and liver and causes other health problems.* 5, 25, 31, 33, 34

ANTIBODIES—*Substances made by blood that fight off foreign organisms.* 20

COCAINE—*A stimulant. This drug excites the body. It speeds up your nervous system and increases the activity of the mind and body.* 7, 9, 12, 14, 17, 18, 19, 24, 25, 27, 33, 37

CRACK—*A powerful form of cocaine that is usually smoked.* 14, 17

DRUG TESTING—*Scientific testing that identifies drugs in urine or blood.* 5, 6, 11, 12, 14, 23, 27, 28, 30, 31, 33, 34, 35, 36, 37, 38, 39, 40, 43, 44

EMPLOYEE ASSISTANCE ROGRAMS—*Programs set up by businesses to prevent drug abuse in the workplace and to help drug abusers.* 43

ENZYME IMMUNOASSAY—*A drug test that separates drugs out of urine. Small urine samples are mixed with antibodies; then light is passed through the samples.*

46

GLOSSARY/INDEX

Color changes tell laboratory workers which drugs are in the urine. 19

GAS CHROMATOGRAPHY/MASS SPECTROM-ETRY—*A test that separates drugs from urine. A urine sample is mixed with gas and special chemicals, then run through a gas chromatograph, which is a large and complex machine. The sample is then run through a mass spectrometer, another costly machine. The urine separates into its different chemicals through the electric forces of the mass spectrometer. Laboratory workers can then tell which drugs are in the urine.* 21

HALLUCINOGENS—*Drugs that produce a variety of vivid sensations and alter mood and thought.* 14, 17

HEROIN—*An opiate. This drug tends to relax the body. Heroin is often smoked, but more often is injected with needles into people's blood vessels.* 6, 9, 11, 17, 18, 24

ILLEGAL—*Against the law.* 5, 6, 7, 9, 11, 20, 22, 23, 24, 25, 27, 31, 33, 34, 36, 40, 44

LSD—*Lysergic acid diethylamide (LSD) is the world's most powerful hallucinogen.* 17

MANDATORY DRUG TESTING—*Drug tests that everyone has to undergo.* 36

MARIJUANA—*A hallucinogen that changes people's moods. It is usually smoked.* 6, 9, 18, 19, 23, 24, 25, 37, 38, 42

OPIATES—*Drugs that cause the body to relax.* 14, 17, 37

GLOSSARY/INDEX

PCP—*Phencyclidine (PCP), or angel dust, is a powerful hallucinogen. 17, 18, 37*

PROBENECID—*A drug that masks anabolic steroids in a drug test. 25*

RADIOACTIVE—*Describes materials that give off radiation. 20*

RADIOIMMUNOASSAY—*A test that identifies drugs in urine. It uses radioactive chemicals attached to antibodies. The antibodies then attach to the drugs. 20*

RANDOM DRUG TESTING—*A program that allows drug testing at any time, without warning. 31, 33, 37, 39, 43*

SEDATIVES—*Drugs that tend to relax the body. 14, 17, 37*

SENSITIVE JOBS—*Jobs that involve the safety and security of others. 39*

STIMULANTS—*Drugs that excite and stimulate the body. They increase the activity of the heart and brain. They are also the largest group of illegal drugs used in America and include cocaine, crack, and amphetamines. 14*

SUBSTANCE ABUSE—*Drug abuse. 41*

THIN LAYER CHROMATOGRAPHY—*A test method to separate drugs from urine. A dot of urine is placed on a thin layer of gel that covers a glass plate. Over time, the spot disappears and a series of spots appear all over the gel. Each spot is a different drug. 20*